Yellow Wolf

Grant Tarbard

Yellow Wolf
Writing Knights Press — Cleveland, Ohio

http://writingknights.com
http://facebook.com/writingknights

ISBN 978-1-50538-356-0

Copyright © 2014 Grant Tarbard

All Rights Reserved. No part of this publication may be reproduced, stored in a retrieval system, or transmitted, in any form or in any means – by electronic, mechanical, photocopying, recording or otherwise – without prior written permission.

To Bethany W. Pope
for her inspiration,
help and friendship.

Hoc autem
quod resurgant

Contents

Assurances / A Sample of Death /
Observing the Sabbath ... 1
A Galaxy of Coils / Lonely Kingdom / Visitation ... 2
Acheron / Beast Milk / Blood on His Chest ... 3
Celibacy / Chasing Butterflies / Consumption ... 4
Contemplation / Drugs / Eucharist ... 5
Family / Feeding / His Black Dog Mood ... 6
Curse / Pledge / Rusty Locket ... 7
Holy Orders / Lights / Martyrs ... 8
Mold / No One / Orthodoxy ... 9
Salt / Seclusion / Security ... 10
Spring / Summer Dusk / Summoning ... 11
Body of the Wolf / First Cut / Ghosts on the Horizon ... 12
Hunter / Landscape of Smoke ... 13
Moulting / Nine Herbs Charm ... 14
The Ringing Bells / Rot / The Stalking Moon ... 15
Uncertainness / Vagrancy / Visions ... 16
Waiting / Wandering / Resurgence ... 17
A Gathering / Folktale / And Glaring Still ... 18
Ashen / Beyond the Pines / Anticipation of the Hunt ... 19
Closed Eyes to the Blur / Wolf's Philosophy / Coil ... 20
Come Back / Blanket / Coup D'etat ... 21
Yellow Wolf on Orange / Cosmos in One /
The Dream Father ... 22
Last of It / The Lost / The Warning ... 23
This Mournful Light / What He Found / Youth ... 24
Sits on Paper Streets / Manicured Grove /
Time Thinks of a Wolf ... 25
Piggies / The Ascent to Heaven ... 26

Assurances

The yellow wolf is
a dust angel with
piranha teeth, his
place in Heaven is
assured by his kills.

A Sample of Death

The yellow wolf, all
bracken, bush and thorns.
Don't look, saluting,
for there is nothing
else to do with Death.

Observing the Sabbath

Sabbath on yellow
wolf's mountain, no false
idols are present.
Ladybird incense
languishes, floating.

A Galaxy of Coils

Yellow wolf is a
galaxy of this
coiled tongue against the
electric fence of
a turpentine kiss.

Lonely Kingdom

Yellow wolf has not
had to say hello,
he is the Alpha,
the Omega of
a lonely kingdom.

Visitation

Yellow wolf reads the
moon and predicts that
the archangel will
visit him tonight.
He never has yet.

Acheron

Yellow wolf lives in
flame, burning down his
rust palace on the
river of woe in
the gloom twist of fate.

Beast Milk

Yellow wolf drinks tea
with milk squeezed from the
angelic breast of
the beast in the woods
whom is but shadow.

Blood on His Chest

Yellow wolf is gripped
to a bloodied phlox
that he keeps as it's
a badge resembling
the unmade bed grave.

Celibacy

The yellow wolf is
not rampant, his lost
passion is on a
trip, packed its Scotchgard
bags and went away.

Chasing Butterflies

The yellow wolf howls
at the bright Zero
butterflies, burning
diesel with every
flutter of the wing.

Consumption

Yellow wolf is dew,
eager in his glow.
Ligament echo,
loam lightning devil,
oak-leaved and aloof.

Contemplation

He, yellow wolf sits
on a mound of ants.
No unkind word will
echo these chambers,
yellowed and sweetened.

Drugs

The yellow wolf has
a fog of ether,
Lidocaine yells at
that sagging belly
sun, dusk embittered.

Eucharist

The yellow wolf saw
giants coming from
the seas, they're going
to put out a bowl
of Eucharist blood.

Family

The yellow wolf has
many family
members: coyote,
hyena, dingo,
fox. They're all dog-toothed.

Feeding

Faceless yellow wolf,
elegant killer
embowels sweet things.
Daemones give feedback
snarling their blessing.

His Black Dog Mood

The yellow wolf, when
he is in a black
dog mood, attacks in
black and white noir with
Cerberus steel teeth.

Curse

Yellow wolf lets out
a pitiful cry,
he's cursed with limbless
oceans of sorrow,
he can't grip the stars.

Pledge

Yellow wolf pledges
he will be naked
in the slight hand of
the labyrinth of
the phonograph dusk.

Rusty Locket

Yellow wolf holds close
the gloom sea's scarlet
furnace in a green,
rusty locket. The
sea is hot blooded.

Holy Orders

Yellow wolf eats his
flesh only when he's
on Holy orders.
He's not sold cheaply,
he's sold by the ounce.

Lights

Yellow wolf thirsts for
solitude, yet he
watches for the car
lights upon the ridge
among the tall pines.

Martyrs

Yellow wolf lives in
the Unmade Forest
and emperors throw
martyrs to him to
glut down their raw bones.

Mold

The yellow wolf has
a tough ruffled hide
of rotten flyers,
free newspapers and
mold ads for dentures.

No One

Yellow wolf sits on
his now cold deck chair,
for it is winter
and the clock ticks for
no one but the dark.

Orthodoxy

Yellow wolf is a
motion of small bone
burials, for in
the Unmade Forest
they are orthodox.

Salt

Yellow wolf is salt
ratified in grain,
a treaty in rock.
He cushions himself
on n a muddy skull.

Seclusion

Yellow wolf sighs, his
look of cobwebs is
a puncture wound in
these blue petals of
his sky solitude.

Security

The yellow wolf has
a matted wad of
keys on a grease chain
around his huge neck.
He keeps what he finds.

Spring

Yellow wolf dances
his old wolf dance
and throws his dread paws
open to welcome
spring's echo vision.

Summer Dusk

Yellow wolf, sun drenched.
There's a musty eve
coming across the
world in a curved arch
with invitation.

Summoning

The yellow wolf is
summoning spirits
of the woodland, he
wears a charm made of
barleycorn in brass.

Body of the Wolf

Yellow wolf, canine
sharp, eats his own flesh.
He starts with the pot
belly, it sags like
an old cardigan.

First Cut

Yellow wolf, frozen
in one point of the
incision, the burnt
crystal blue reaping
of a killers joy.

Ghosts on the Horizon

Yellow wolf glances
over the naked
horizon for a
spot of his long dead
lover, a ghost thread.

Hunter

(I)

Yellow wolf paces
invader footfalls
from the death hunter
into the Unmade
Forest, leaves sing out.

(II)

Yellow wolf, the scent:
transient horror of
the woven hunter
into the Unmade
Forest. Leaves lament.

Landscape of Smoke

The yellow wolf shuns
big cities and smoke.
Landscape of the fox,
scavengers at those
midnight black bin bags.

Moulting

Yellow wolf wants to
be held in the tight
arms of summer clothes,
this moulting dances
in the last snowflakes.

Nine Herbs Charm

(I)

The yellow wolf hides
under a fungus
thorn tree, under dry
Leaves. Stinging nettles are
His patch work blanket.

(II)

The yellow wolf, he
attracts Angel Shades
with his sighing, this
rotten apple core
dispels infection.

The Ringing Bells

Yellow wolf, rough tongued,
bestial, translucent
in soundless woods, a
ghost departing in
the bastard bell skies.

Rot

Yellow wolf attacks.
Blood is on his paws,
haemoglobin made
of these rotting years,
wasted and stolen.

The Stalking Moon

The yellow wolf is
liquid, merging from
the blackened tarmac,
distracting sentries.
At dusk he works best.

Uncertainness

Yellow wolf, bent with
age, roots uncertain.
He's an aurora,
aluminium,
of canned brute red light.

Vagrancy

Yellow wolf is a
hermit of the woods,
a vagrant of his
black skull eyes, away
from the moving stairs.

Visions

The yellow wolf is
hallucinating
the burning of once
lightning torsos that
were his nowhere-friends.

Waiting

The yellow wolf is
still waiting for the
coming Christ, he's got
his Christmas lights hung
up to welcome Him.

Wandering

The yellow wolf was
a refugee from
his broken forest
of glass trees, painted
wanderer's colours.

Resurgence

Wolf can live reeking
of death, it seeps through
his garments on to
the cushion under
his posterior.

A Gathering

Deep in the garden
there is a rock pool
where colours gather
in the dead of night,
hill water skimming.

Folktale

Yellow wolf gnaws bone,
chews down to the song
secured with tendons
that sing like harp strings
when plucked with a seed.

And Glaring Still

Tonight, there are split
cloud bursts across a
patchwork denim sky,
wolf shuts his eyes and
the Moon's rid of him.

Ashen

These leaf stubs sort out
wolf's days, it could be
a month the trees say.
All the lost goodbyes
eat his past with ash.

Beyond the Pines

Wolf ingests blindly,
he's to the marrow
of all consuming
life beyond the pines,
seduced by the soil.

Anticipation
of the Hunt

The poring rain melts
a heart not dusted
for musty finger
prints. A blood breathing
anticipation.

Closed Eyes
to the Blur

Wolf's the ghost in his
own story, the blur
on the edge of the
photograph at all
the glitter parties.

Wolf's Philosophy

"A crimson tulip
life isn't worth living
if you don't love with
awe in your bowels,
intestines are love".

Coil

Wolf's mortality
defines his spirit,
death comes to us all.
Wolf's existence, just
soil in the ground.

Come Back

Wolf's digging a hole
to bury crow in,
down to the Earth's core.
"You've become grotesque,
come home repaired".

Blanket

The yellow wolf has
flame spiders lying
down on a blanket
of cobwebs. He traps
them to be his light.

Coup D'etat

The yellow wolf digs
at something deep and
dark. A stump on a
knoll ignored, his stale
awe shook the timbers.

Yellow Wolf on Orange

Yellow wolf, naked
in midnight's blood of
orange sepia.
He howl's as he has
nothing else to do.

Cosmos in One

The yellow wolf stalls
at an entrance to
a cave of green moss,
stalactites dripping
the drop of aeons.

The Dream Father

The yellow wolf, you
never grew to be
a father, this dream
has died to be a
secret wrapped in leaves.

Last of It

Yellow wolf feasts on
an apple, mourning
nothing except the
last soil visions that
he's had all along.

The Lost

Yellow wolf burns a
rotten newspaper
boat, an effigy
to the lost poets.
Their art died with them.

The Warming

The yellow wolf skulks
around his dried up
shortcrust rime riverbed
remembering a
lucid aqua dream.

This Mournful Light

The yellow wolf holds
sacred these full beams,
in darkness he is
poor but proud of his
mournful lantern light.

What He Found

Yellow wolf wears a
yellow star, reeking
with meaning, though not
to him. He found it
in a dream of leaves.

Youth

Yellow wolf is his
ancient Régime.
Made of dust matted
from centuries worth
of Hell's camp fire soot.

Sits on Paper Streets

On outskirts pre-loved
by a lampshade's bulb
burning paper streets,
yellow wolf is the
town's second father.

Manicured Grove

Deliberate lines,
trees in a high grove
cut by razor wire.
There, wolves say sorry
so beautifully.

Time Thinks of a Wolf

And when yellow wolf
thinks of the world he
shudders within a
crumbling dust jacket
of powdered clock ticks.

Piggies

Pigs slam their mucky
straw doors on him, he's
not got the puff to
blow their houses in,
wolf will meet you there.

The Ascent to Heaven

Wolf's eyes close as the
abattoir sun sets
on a cold grey dawn,
pissing on the soil
carpet of the earth.

Thanks to Christy Miron,
Assistant Editor
of Postcards, Poems and Prose
for publishing:
'His Black Dog Mood',
Consumption'
and 'This Mournful Light',
the first 'Yellow Wolf poems
to be published.

Some 'Yellow Wolf' 5x5's
have appeared in The Screech Owl.

Print Titles Available through Writing Knights Press

The Squire: Page-A-Day Anthology 2015
Unbound — Lorraine Cipriano
According to the Results — Alexis-Rueal
Piercing Words …from the Heart — Diwakar Pokhriyal
Little Sister — Ruth Morris
I See Things are Falling (2nd Edition) — Kathleen D. Gallagher
Absent Meteors (2nd Edition) — Steve Brightman
Cannibal Sunflowers (2nd Edition) — Catfish McDaris
Arrival and Departure — James Schwartz
So Careless of Themselves — Lennart Lundh
Love, Unwrapped (2nd Edition) — Mandy Buffington
Thieves in the Wind — Subhankar Das & Catfish McDaris
In the Beginning and the End (2nd Edition) — Siddartha Beth Pierce
Bluebird Don't Mean Nothing — David Mac
The Squire: Scare Me
Lucid Brightenings — Jen Pezzo
Last Chance for Rain — Sharon Frye
200 Years — Serena Castells
The Squire: National Poetry Month Anthology (2013)
Nothing, but Skin — Quartez Harris
Johnny Badge — Jnana Hodson
Escape to Cyberspace — Gary Beck
Life After Checkmate — Andrew Line
Menthol Slims One-Twenty Blues — Walter Beck
The Gospel of Flies — Bethany W. Pope
The Squire: Karma & Renewal
Zoptic Figure — Jeff Kosiba
"don't buy this" — Azriel Johnson
Eating Yellow Snow — Phoenix Clouden
The Squire: Grand Tournament 2 Anthology
The Squire: Warriors Anthology
Graffiti Wisdom — Skylark Bruce
The Squire: Seasons Anthology
Writing Knights Press 2012 Anthology
The Squire: Hands Anthology
The Squire: Grand Tournament Anthology
Writing Knights Press Best of 2011 Anthology

Printed in Poland
by Amazon Fulfillment
Poland Sp. z o.o., Wrocław